MAILBOX
The Education Center

Dianne Sw

grades

Graphic Organizers

Over 50 Easy-to-Adapt Organizers That Help Students

- Make Predictions
- Compare and Contrast
- Explore Story Elements
- Summarize
- Sequence Events

- Determine Cause and Effect
- Build Vocabulary
- Make Decisions
- Plan and Organize
- Collect Data

And Much, Much More!

Improve reading and writing skills!

Written by Kim Minafo

Managing Editor: Hope Taylor Spencer

Editorial Team: Becky S. Andrews, Kimberley Bruck, Karen P. Shelton, Diane Badden, Thad H. McLaurin, Debra Liverman, Sherry McGregor, Amy Payne, Karen A. Brudnak, Sarah Hamblet, Hope Rodgers, Dorothy C. McKinney

Production Team: Lisa K. Pitts, Pam Crane, Rebecca Saunders, Jennifer Tipton Cappoen, Chris Curry, Sarah Foreman, Theresa Lewis Goode, Clint Moore, Greg D. Rieves, Barry Slate, Donna K. Teal, Zane Williard, Tazmen Carlisle, Marsha Heim, Amy Kirtley-Hill, Cathy Edwards Simrell, Lynette Dickerson, Mark Rainey

www.themailbox.com

Table of Contents

©2006 The Mailbox®
All rights reserved.
ISBN10 #1-56234-694-6 • ISBN13 #978-156234-694-2

Manufactured in the United States
10 9 8 7 6 5 4 3 2

How to Use

1. Scan the table of contents to find just the right organizer to meet your objectives.

2. Read the accompanying teacher page for simple directions on how to complete the organizer and use it in several different curriculum areas.

3. Make copies of the organizer for your students.

Teacher Page

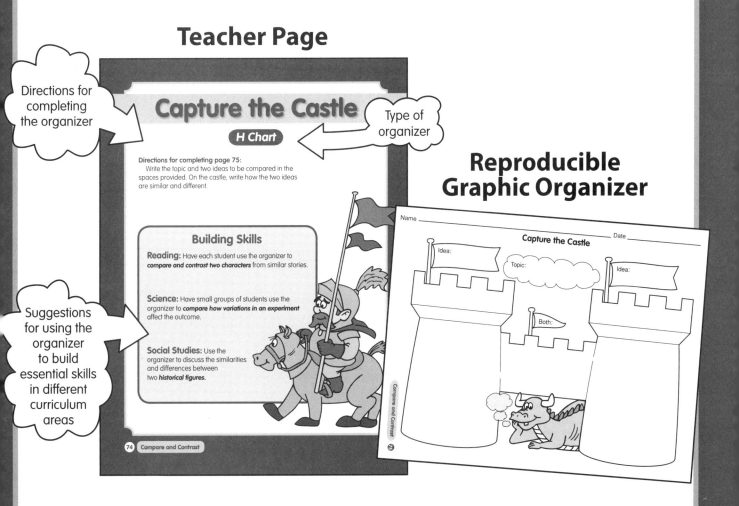

Directions for completing the organizer

Type of organizer

Suggestions for using the organizer to build essential skills in different curriculum areas

Capture the Castle
H Chart

Directions for completing page 75:
Write the topic and two ideas to be compared in the spaces provided. On the castle, write how the two ideas are similar and different.

Building Skills

Reading: Have each student use the organizer to *compare and contrast two characters* from similar stories.

Science: Have small groups of students use the organizer to *compare how variations in an experiment* affect the outcome.

Social Studies: Use the organizer to discuss the similarities and differences between two *historical figures.*

74 Compare and Contrast

Reproducible Graphic Organizer

Name _____ Date _____

Capture the Castle

Idea: _____   Topic: _____   Idea: _____

Both: _____

Compare and Contrast

Lighting the Way

KWL chart

Directions for completing page 5:

1. Write the topic.
2. Write what you already know about the topic in the first column.
3. Write what you want to know about the topic in the second column.
4. Read the text.
5. Write what you have learned about the topic in the third column.

Building Skills

Writing: On her next *research assignment,* have each student complete the organizer and narrow her topic by circling two or three key ideas she would like to find out more about.

Reading: Have each student use the organizer before, while, and after she reads a chapter in a *chapter book.*

Social Studies: Create a transparency of the organizer and use it to *introduce a new unit.*

Name _____

Date _____

Lighting the Way

Topic: _____

K What I Know	W What I Want to Know	L What I Learned

Knock, Knock

KWS chart

Directions for completing page 7:

1. Write the topic.
2. On the first door, write what you already know about the topic.
3. On the second door, write what you would like to learn about the topic.
4. On the third door, write possible sources where information about the topic may be found.

Building Skills

Writing: Before they write a *biography,* have students use the chart to organize ideas and sources about the person they're researching.

Science: Have students complete the organizer to prepare for a *science fair project or report.*

Social Studies: Use the organizer with students before exploring a new *social studies topic.*

Name _____

Knock, Knock

Opening doors to _____
topic

Possible Sources

What I **W**ant to Know

What I **K**now

©The Mailbox® • *Graphic Organizers* • TEC60995

Bubbling Over

Directions for completing page 9:

Fill in each bubble to show what you think the reading will be about. Then write your prediction on the bathtub.

Building Skills

Reading: Have small groups of students *gather information* and then fill in the bubbles before reading a book together.

Reading: Have students use the organizer when reading children's *newsmagazines.*

Reading: Create a transparency of the organizer and use it as a *discussion starter* before you begin your next read-aloud session. Then revisit student predictions during reading.

Bubbles, Bubbles

Name_____   Date _____

Bubbling Over

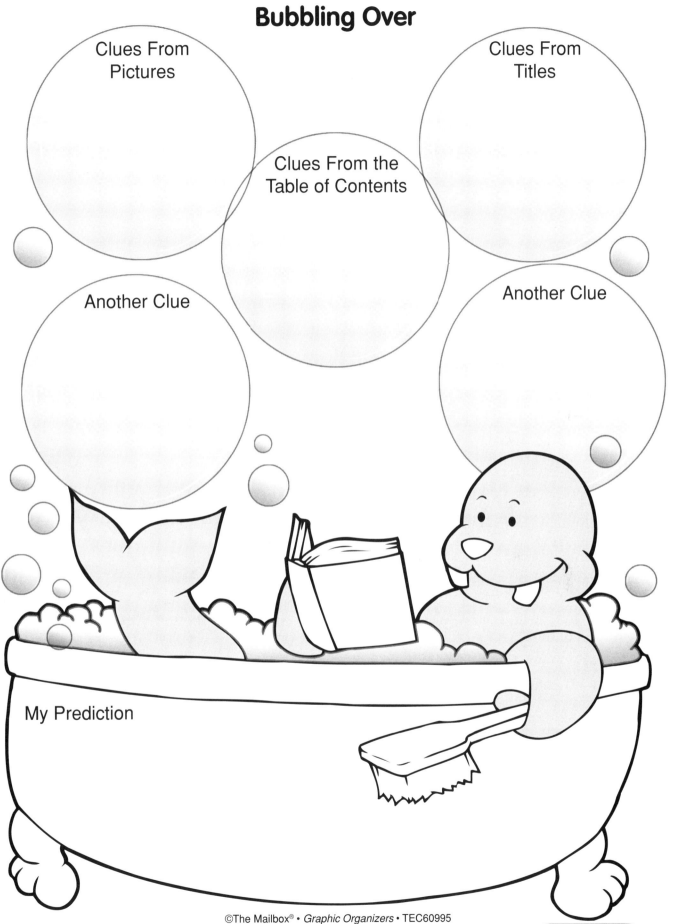

Clues From
Pictures

Clues From the
Table of Contents

Clues From
Titles

Another Clue

Another Clue

My Prediction

©The Mailbox® • *Graphic Organizers* • TEC60995

Prereading 9

Growth Spurt

Prediction chart

Directions for completing page 11:

1. Preview the story.
2. Next to the first column, label each sign with one of the following: "plot," "setting," "characters," and "author's purpose."
3. In the first column, write your predictions for each topic.
4. In the second column, write your reasons for each prediction.
5. After reading the text, use the third column to compare your predictions to what actually happened.
6. In the last column, write what you learned from your predictions.

Building Skills

Reading: Use the graphic organizer to help students **preview and review chapters** in a chapter book.

Reading: Have students complete the organizer to **compare different books** read over a period of time.

Science: Record students' **predictions and observations for science experiments** on the graphic organizer.

Name _____   Date _____

Growth Spurt

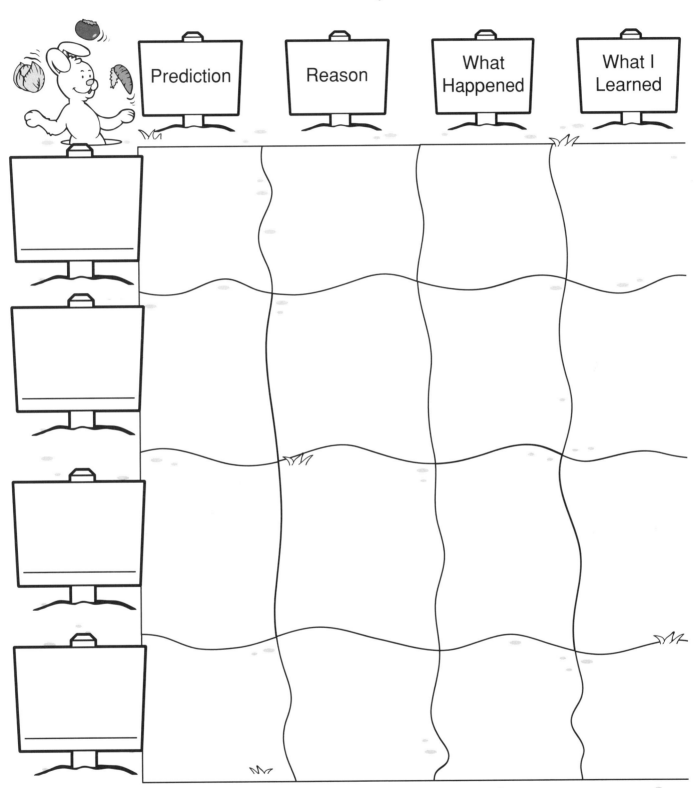

Prediction   Reason   What Happened   What I Learned

Paint the Town!

Forecasting chart

Directions for completing page 13:
Write the topic or title and then answer each question.

Building Skills

Writing: Have each student use the organizer to plan and write a **persuasive paragraph.**

Reading: Use the organizer to help students document a **character's conflict** in a story and plan advice that could help solve the character's problem.

Science: Have each student use the organizer to explore an **environmental issue.**

Name_____ Date _____

Paint the Town!

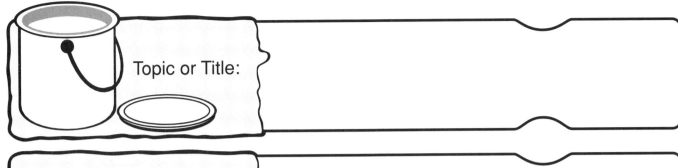

Topic or Title:

What is the problem?

What is a possible effect of the problem?

What is another possible effect?

What could change the possible outcomes?

What should the plan of action be?

Looking Sharp!

Beginning, middle, and end

Directions for completing page 15:

1. Record the title on the turtle's hat.
2. In the first section, write about the beginning.
3. In the bottom section, write about the end.
4. In the middle section, write about what happens between the beginning and the end.

Building Skills

Writing: Have students **plan a narrative** using the organizer.

Reading: Guide students to use the organizer to **take notes** as they read. Then have them use the notes to summarize their reading.

Science: Use the organizer to teach students to **record the steps in a science experiment.**

Name _____   Date _____

Looking Sharp!

Title:

Beginning:

Middle:

End:

Action!

Filmstrip organizer

Directions for completing page 17:
1. Write about the beginning in the first part.
2. Write about the middle in the center part.
3. Write about the end in the last part.
4. Fill in the remaining parts with other important events.

Building Skills

Writing: Use the organizer to help students plan a *narrative writing piece.*

Reading: Use the organizer to help students *analyze* the way *a character* changes.

Speaking: Guide students to plan *class presentations* with the organizer.

Name _____ Date _____

Action!

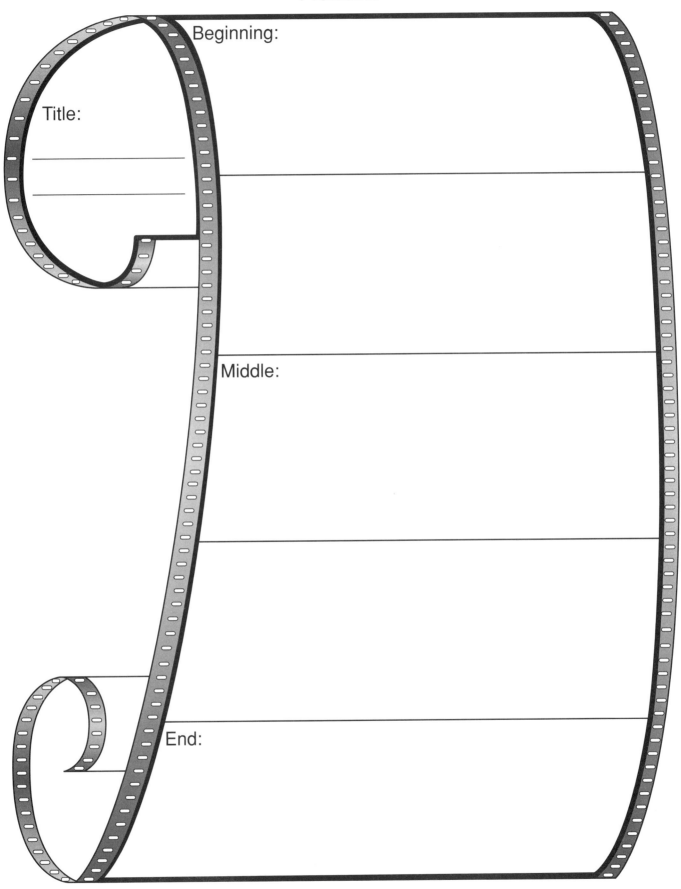

Title:

_____

_____

Beginning:

Middle:

End:

Follow the Bouncing Ball!

Flowchart

Directions for completing page 19:
   Write the main events in order. Review to make sure you listed only the most important things.

Building Skills

Reading: Use the chart to help a student organize her thoughts for a *summary* of a reading passage.

Writing: Have students use the organizer to *plan a trip* to their favorite vacation spot.

Social Studies: Have students use the flowchart to *sequence the major events* of a historical period.

Name _____ Date _____

Follow the Bouncing Ball!

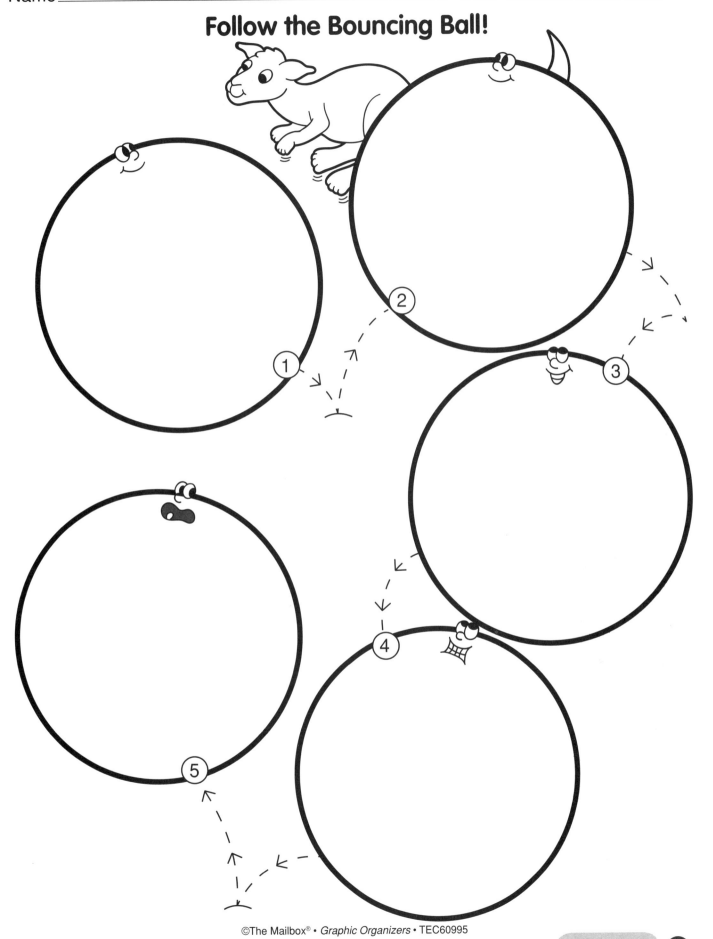

Turn, Turn

Sequence circle

Directions for completing page 21:

Write the topic in the center circle. Then use words and pictures to show each event in the cycle.

Building Skills

Writing: Guide students to use the organizer to **plan an essay** that explains how to complete a repetitive task such as making a greeting card.

Reading: Have students use the organizer to **analyze a story's problem.**

Science: Have students **illustrate the water cycle or a plant's or an animal's life cycle** using this organizer.

Name_____ Date_____

Turn, Turn

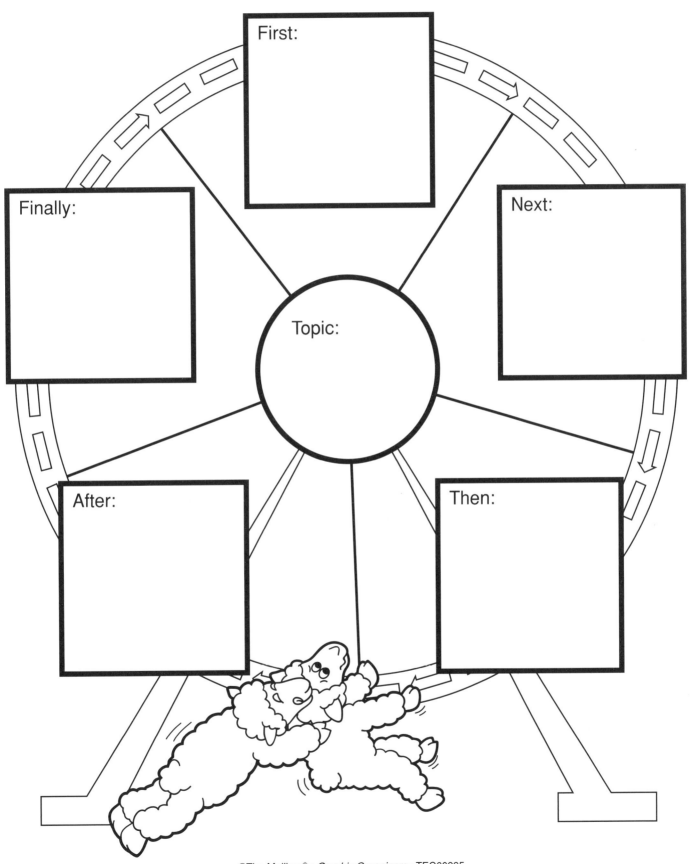

First:

Finally:

Topic:

Next:

After:

Then:

Leaf by Leaf

Storyboard

Directions for completing page 23:

1. Record the topic or story title on the stem.
2. Draw a picture of the main event that begins the story in the first leaf.
3. Illustrate the main event that ends the story in the last leaf.
4. In the remaining leaves, add pictures that describe the other important parts of the story.
5. Make sure your pictures retell the story in order.

Building Skills

Writing: Have each student use the organizer to write a **personal narrative.** Guide her to choose an event and then illustrate an important detail in each space.

Reading: Read a story aloud. Have each student complete a storyboard independently and then direct students to **compare** their **retellings.**

Math: Have students use the organizer to show the steps in solving an **addition or subtraction problem with regrouping.**

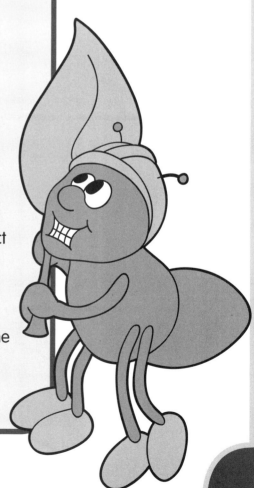

Name _____

Date _____

Leaf by Leaf

First:

Second:

Third:

Topic: _____

Fourth:

Fifth:

Sixth:

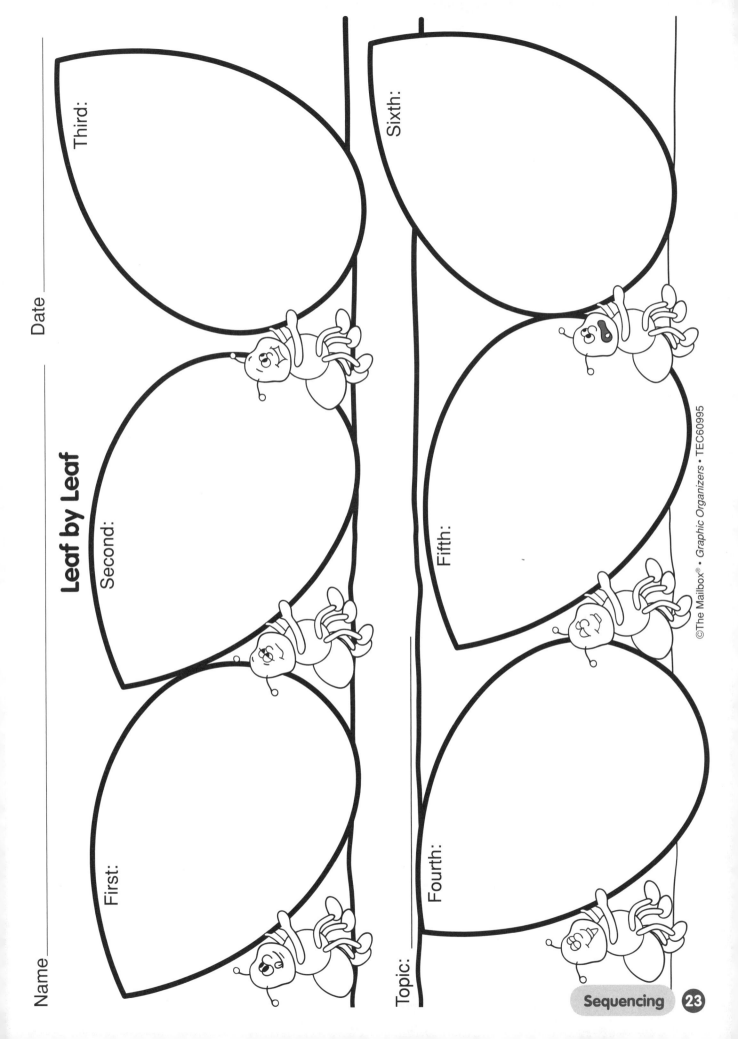

Keep Me Posted!

Timeline

Directions for completing page 25:
Write each important event and its date in order.

Building Skills

Writing: Use the organizer to guide each student to brainstorm six important events in his life and then write a *personal narrative.*

Writing: Have students use the organizer to take notes about a famous person. Then have each student use her notes to write a *biographical report.*

Social Studies: Project a transparency of the organizer and have students help you sequence the details of an *important historical event* or period of time that you've been learning about.

Name _____ Date _____

Keep Me Posted!

Title:

First Event:

Date:

Date: Second Event:

Third Event:

Date:

Date: Fourth Event:

Fifth Event:

Date:

Date: Sixth Event:

Buggy About a Great Idea!

E chart

Directions for completing page 27:
Write the main idea where indicated. Then write each supporting detail where indicated.

Building Skills

Writing: Have students use the organizer to plan an **expository paragraph** about a nonfiction topic.

Writing: Have students use the organizer to plan a **personal narrative.**

Reading: Have students use the organizer to separate the **main idea** from its supporting details while reading.

Buggy About a Great Idea!

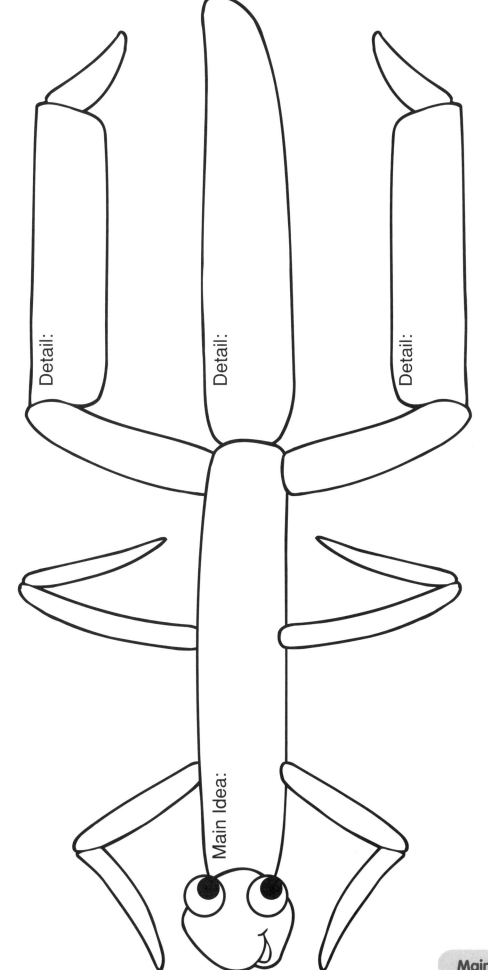

Detail:

Detail:

Detail:

Main Idea:

Main Idea **27**

For Good Measure!

Idea web

Directions for completing page 29:
  Write the main idea on the bowl. Then write each supporting detail on a measuring cup.

Building Skills

Writing: Create a transparency of the organizer. Use it to model *story idea webs* with topics such as caring for a pet or playing a sport.

Reading: Have students use the organizer to record and sort information from a *nonfiction passage* they are reading.

Social Studies: Have students use the organizer to gather ideas for a *social studies report*.

Name _____

Date _____

For Good Measure!

Main Idea:

Detail:

Detail:

Detail:

Detail:

©The Mailbox® • *Graphic Organizers* • TEC60995

Main Idea 29

Sweet Reward

Main idea pyramid

Directions for completing page 31:

1. Write the topic.
2. Write the main idea.
3. In the boxes below the main idea, write four different details that each support the main idea.

Building Skills

Writing: Use the organizer to help students plan a *descriptive paragraph.*

Reading: Have students use the page to analyze a *character's actions.* Direct each student to write the character's name in the "Topic" box and then describe a problem related to the character in the "Main Idea" box. Next, have him record details about the character's actions or reactions to the problem in the "Detail" boxes.

Reading: Have students write a *story's setting* in the topic box, write a sentence describing the setting in the main idea box, and then write details that support the description in each detail box.

Name _____ Date _____

Sweet Reward

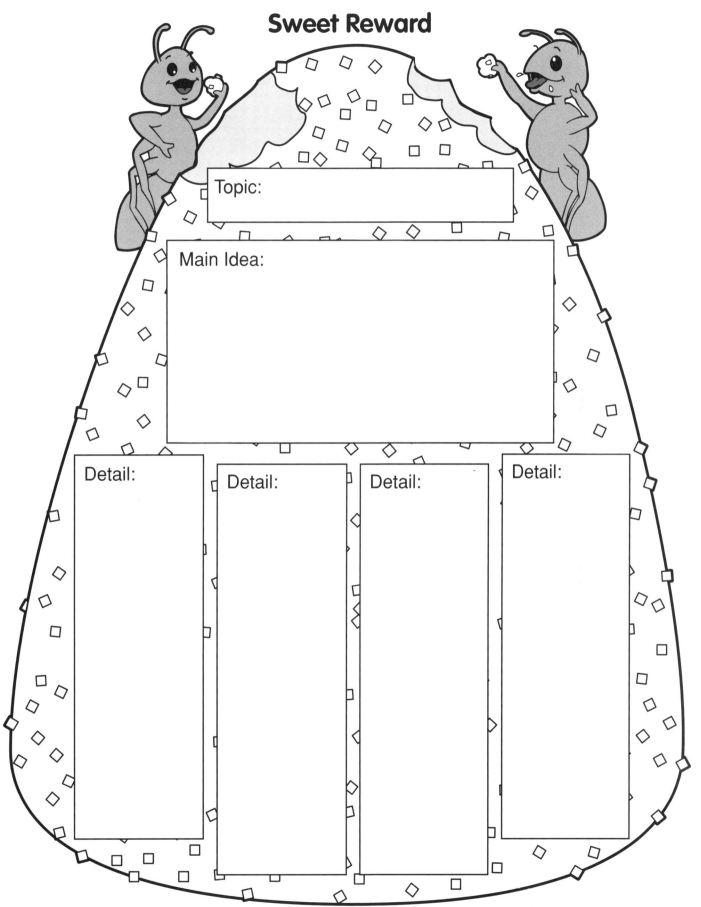

Topic:

Main Idea:

Detail:

Detail:

Detail:

Detail:

Main Idea 31

Take a Leafy Look!

Fishbone web

Directions for completing page 33:

Write a statement about the main idea where indicated. Then write each detail along the leaf's veins.

Building Skills

Writing: Have students use the organizer to plan their own **nonfiction paragraphs.**

Social Studies: Make a transparency of the organizer and use it with your class after reading about a **current event** in an age-appropriate newspaper article or a weekly student newsmagazine.

Reading: Use the organizer as a pre-reading or post-reading tool for **nonfiction text.**

Take a Leafy Look!

Main Idea:

Supreme Summary

Summarizing chart

Directions for completing page 35:
Write the title. On each oven door, summarize the events from the story in order.

Building Skills

Writing: Use the organizer to help students plan a *personal narrative* about going out to eat at a fun restaurant.

Writing: Have each student use the organizer to write directions for creating his *favorite meal.*

Social Studies: Create a transparency of the organizer. At the end of class, use the organizer to review and summarize *important information* learned that day.

Name _____ Date _____

Supreme Summary

_____
title

First:

Then:

Next:

After that:

Finally:

Summarizing 35

Treasure Hunt

Chapter map

Directions for completing page 37:

Write the title of the book on the treasure chest. Then complete each section of the map.

Building Skills

Reading: Create a transparency of the organizer and use it with the class as a *chapter review.*

Reading: Prior to reading, use the organizer to discuss the *elements of a story.* Then, after reading, have students complete the page as directed above.

Reading: Have students use the organizer to help them summarize a *current events article.*

Name _____ Date _____

Treasure Hunt

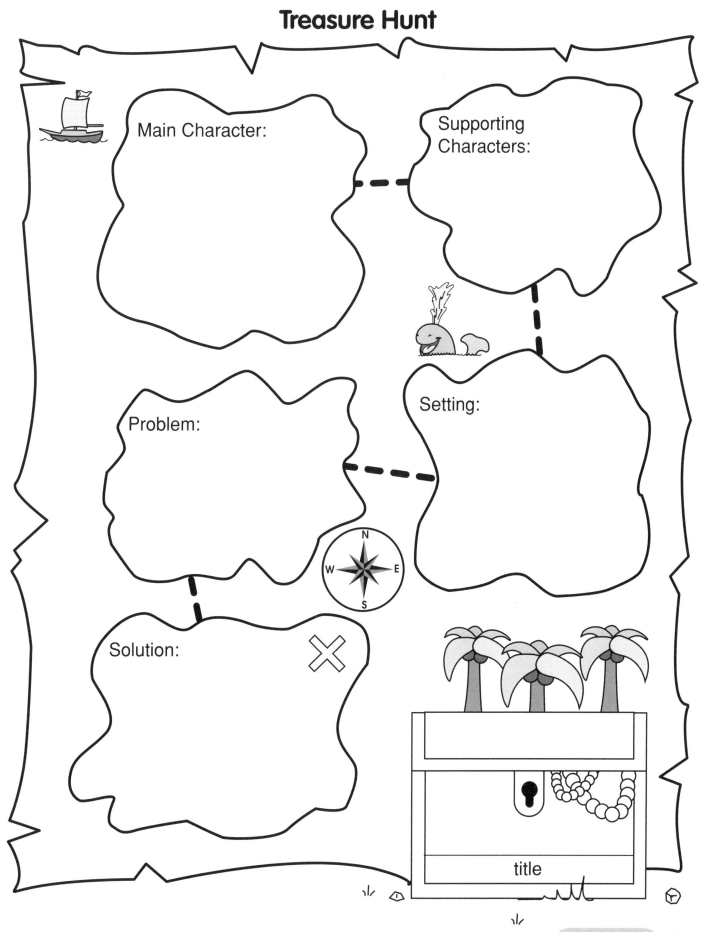

Main Character:

Supporting Characters:

Problem:

Setting:

Solution:

title

Hats Off!

Story notes

Directions for completing page 39:
Write the title and author. Then fill in each labeled hat to summarize an element from the story.

Building Skills

Writing: Have each student use the organizer as a *prewriting tool* before beginning a story draft.

Reading: Use the organizer to help students prepare for *oral book reports*.

Social Studies: Have each student complete the organizer to summarize or analyze an important *historical event*.

Name_____ Date _____

Hats Off!

_____   _____
title   author

Setting:

Character:

Character:

Problem:

Important Event:

Theme or Message:

Windmill of Wonder

Who, what, when, where, why, and how web

Directions for completing page 41:
Write the title. Then answer each question.

Building Skills

Writing: Use the organizer as a **brainstorming** activity prior to writing a story.

Reading: Have each student complete the organizer after reading a **nonfiction article.**

Science: Use the organizer to introduce or review **famous scientists** and their contributions to the field.

Name_____ Date _____

Windmill of Wonder

_____
title

When?

Who?

What?

Where?

Why? How?

Clowning Around

Character comparison chart

Directions for completing page 43:

1. Write a different character's name on each blank.
2. Record words and phrases that show differences between the two characters in the space below each name.
3. Record similarities between the characters in the space where the two circles overlap.

Building Skills

Reading: Create a transparency of the organizer and use it to **compare two characters** from different stories.

Reading: Pair students and have each pair use the organizer to **compare a specific trait, action, or feeling** of two characters.

Science: Have each student use the organizer to **compare the lives or contributions** of two different scientists or inventors.

Name _____

Clowning Around

Character

Both

Character

Story Elements 43

Lights, Camera, Action!

Character web

Directions for completing page 45:
Fill in each section of the camera with information about one character from the story. Then draw a picture of the character in the space provided.

Building Skills

Writing: Have small groups of students use the organizer to develop a fictional character for a *narrative-writing* assignment.

Reading: Have each student use two copies of the organizer to *compare a book and movie version of a character.*

Name _____

Lights, Camera, Action!

What the character looks like:

character

Words to describe the character's personality or attitude:

Picture of the character:

Story Elements **45**

A Pair of Views

Character perspective chart

Directions for completing page 47:

   Write a main event from the story on the fruit bowl. Then, on each piece of fruit, write a character's name. Tell how each character might view the event.

Building Skills

Writing: Have each student complete the organizer to evaluate two sides of an argument before ***writing a persuasive essay.***

Reading: Use the organizer to ***compare the ideas or opinions*** of two different characters from the same story.

Social Studies: Have small groups of students use the organizer to ***compare two different people's views*** about the same historical event.

Name _____

Date _____

A Pair of Views

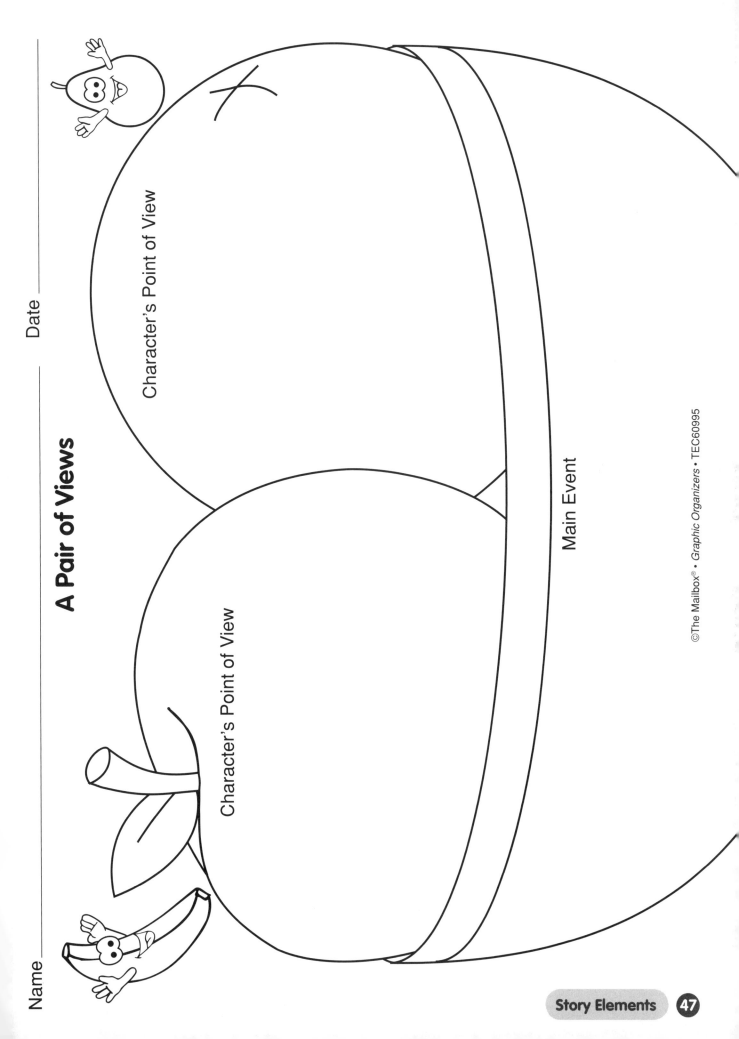

Character's Point of View

Character's Point of View

Main Event

Story Elements **47**

Seaside

Sociogram

Directions for completing page 49:

Write the name of the main character on the hermit crab. Then, on each additional sea creature, write the name of a character and his or her relationship to the main character.

Building Skills

Writing: Have each student use the organizer to **plan character relationships** before writing a narrative story.

Reading: Provide each student with two copies of the graphic organizer. Have her **compare the character relationships** at the **beginning of the story** on the first organizer and their relationships at the **end of the story** on the second organizer.

Seaside

_____
character

_____
main character

_____
character

Snack Bar Similarities

Personal connection chart

Directions for completing page 51:
1. Record the title and author of the story.
2. In the first column, compare this story to another story that you have read.
3. In the second column, compare this story to something that has happened to you.
4. In the third column, compare this story to something that has happened in the world.

Building Skills

Writing: Have each student use the organizer to *plan a comparison essay.*

Reading: Before reading a nonfiction article, present students with a theme from the article. Then use a transparency of the organizer as a *prereading activity.*

Social Studies: Have small groups of students use the organizer to *make connections to a current event in a news article.*

Name _____

Date _____

Snack Bar Similarities

Text to Text

Text to Self

Text to World

title _____

author _____

Story Elements **51**

Sky High

Plot diagram

Directions for completing page 53:

Write the main events from the story in each corresponding section.

Building Skills

Reading: Have small groups of students practice *sequencing the main events* of a story by labeling small sticky notes and arranging them on a copy of the organizer.

Reading: Encourage each student to use the organizer to *retell a short story.*

Social Studies: Have each student use the organizer to review the important elements of a *historical event.*

Sky High

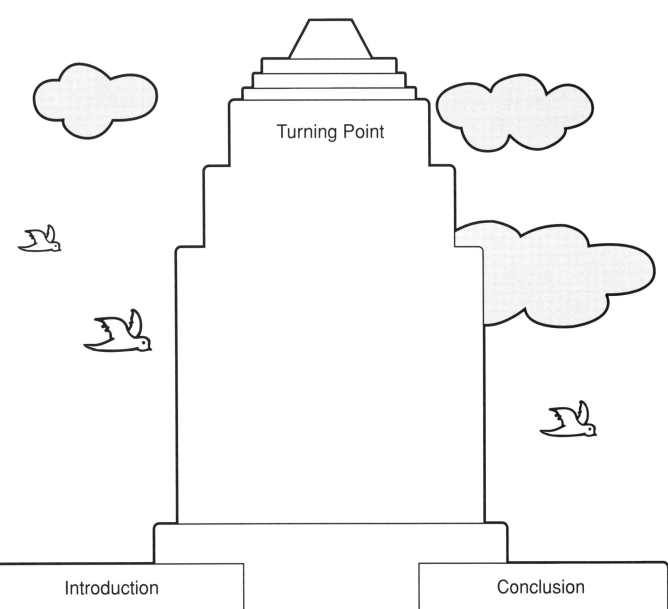

Turning Point

Introduction

Conclusion

Bowl-a-rama

Problem-and-solution diagram

Directions for completing page 55:

Write the character's name and the problem she faces in the space provided. Then write the solution to the problem in the bowling ball.

Building Skills

Reading: Before reading the conclusion to a story, have students use the organizer to **predict** how a character might solve the problem she faces.

Reading: Have a student use the organizer to show a character's **problem and solution.** Then, in the three smaller bowling pins, have the student identify three events that caused the problem.

Social Studies: Use the organizer to teach **social skills.** When a student has a problem at school, have her first write the problem in the large bowling pin. Then have her identify three possible solutions in the smaller bowling pins. Have her write her final choice in the bowling ball.

Name _____ Date _____

Bowl-a-rama

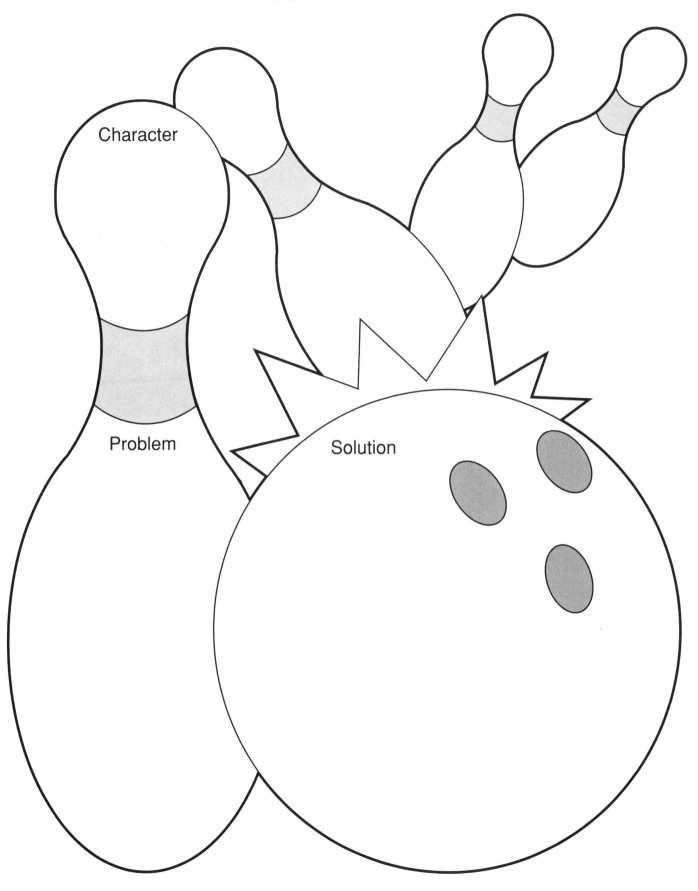

Character

Problem

Solution

Slam Dunk!

Story map

Directions for completing page 57:
Write the title and author of the story. Then complete each section of the basketball.

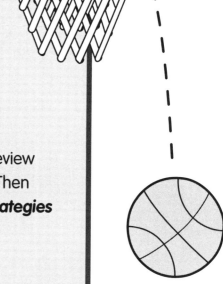

Building Skills

Reading: Have each student use the organizer to **plan a story** for a wordless picture book.

Reading: Use a transparency of the organizer to review a story with a strong problem-and-solution structure. Then brainstorm a list of other possible **problem-solving strategies** the characters in the story could have used.

Math: Have small groups of students use the organizer to plan original **word problems and solutions.**

Name _____ Date _____

Slam Dunk!

title

author

Setting Characters

Problem Solution

Story Elements 57

Spinning a Tale

Story star

Directions for completing page 59:

Write the title of the story on the spider. Then complete each section of the web using information from the story.

Building Skills

Writing: Use the organizer to *plan an original fable.*

Reading: Have students use the organizer to *recall information* from a story that has been read aloud to them.

Social Studies: Have each student use the organizer to record *key information* from a newspaper article or magazine article.

Spinning a Tale

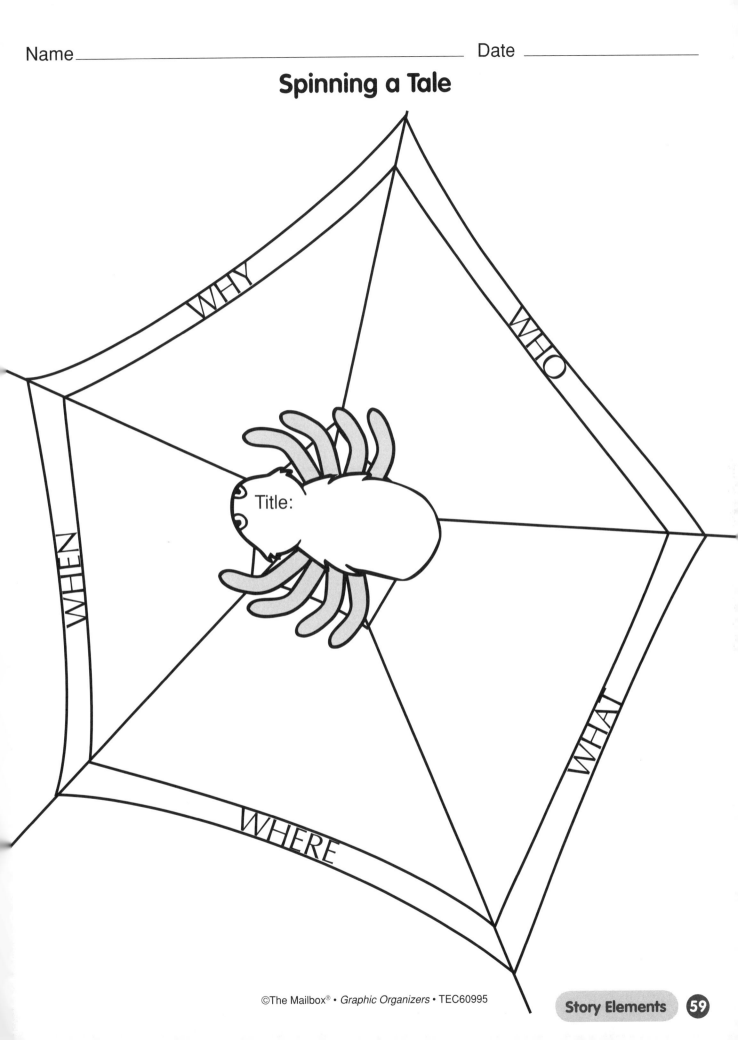

WHY

WHO

WHEN

Title:

WHAT

WHERE

Story Elements 59

Setting the Scene

Setting web

Directions for completing page 61:

Complete each section of the organizer to describe the setting of the story. Then draw a picture of the setting in the window.

Building Skills

Writing: Have each student use the organizer to establish a setting before writing a *narrative story.*

Reading: Have small groups of students *compare settings across texts* by sorting completed organizers based on the time of year, season, location, etc.

Social Studies: Have pairs or small groups of students use the organizer to help them plan and prepare for a *reenactment of a historic event* the class has studied.

Name _____ Date _____

Setting the Scene

Season:

Weather:

Time/Date:

Place:

Surroundings:

Delivery!

Supporting a theme chart

Directions for completing page 63:

1. Before reading, make a prediction about the story's theme by skimming the pages and looking at any available pictures or illustrations. Write your prediction in the top pizza box.
2. Record on the second box at least one example that supports your prediction.
3. After reading the story, check whether your prediction was correct or incorrect in the third pizza box.
4. Write the actual theme of the story on the fourth box. Then, in the last box, provide at least one example that supports the actual theme.

Building Skills

Reading: Display a transparency of the organizer. *Preview an unfamiliar picture book* with your students. Have your students help you complete the organizer; then discuss why their predictions may have been correct or incorrect.

Reading: Use the organizer to help students **make and compare predictions** about a story's theme. Pair students. Give each pair one picture book and two copies of the organizer. Have each student complete his organizer independently. Next, direct the pair to read the book together. Then have the students **compare** their organizers to see whether they had similar **predictions.**

Social Studies: Use the organizer with your students to preview and predict the theme for a picture book about a **historical event** or time period that you are currently studying.

Delivery!

My prediction about the theme:

Example to support my prediction:

My prediction was

☐ correct   ☐ incorrect

Actual theme:

Example to support the actual theme:

Brush It On!

Cause-and-effect chart

Directions for completing page 65:

Write each cause on a paintbrush handle. Then write its effect on the brush.

Building Skills

Writing: Have students use the organizer to plan story events for a **narrative.**

Reading: Help students **identify the effect** first by asking, "What happened?" Then guide them to **determine the cause** by asking, "Why did it happen?"

Social Studies: Guide each student to identify three **community careers** and then list a way each job affects the community.

Name_____   Date _____

Brush It On!

Effect:

Cause:

Effect:

Cause:

Effect:

Cause:

Cause and Effect 65

Fancy Footwork

Chain of events chart

Directions for completing page 67:

1. Write the starting event in the first space.
2. In the second space, write about what the first event caused.
3. In the third space, write about the second event's outcome.

Building Skills

Reading: Guide students to identify a selection's **main event** and the minor events that caused it.

Science: Use the organizer to have students describe a **science process** or experiment.

Social Studies: Have students use the organizer to describe how your **community** was founded.

Name_____ Date _____

Fancy Footwork

Topic: _____

The First Event

The first event caused

Which caused

Arcade Antics

Flowchart

Directions for completing page 69:

1. List the topic.
2. Write details about the first event.
3. Write about what the first event caused.
4. Write about what the second event caused.
5. Write about what finally happened.

Building Skills

Writing: Guide students to plan a *humorous narrative* by filling out the chart backward.

Writing: To plan a *how-to paragraph,* have the student list each action that leads to the next step or action.

Reading: Have students use the form to *take notes* during a read-aloud.

Name _____ Date _____

Arcade Antics

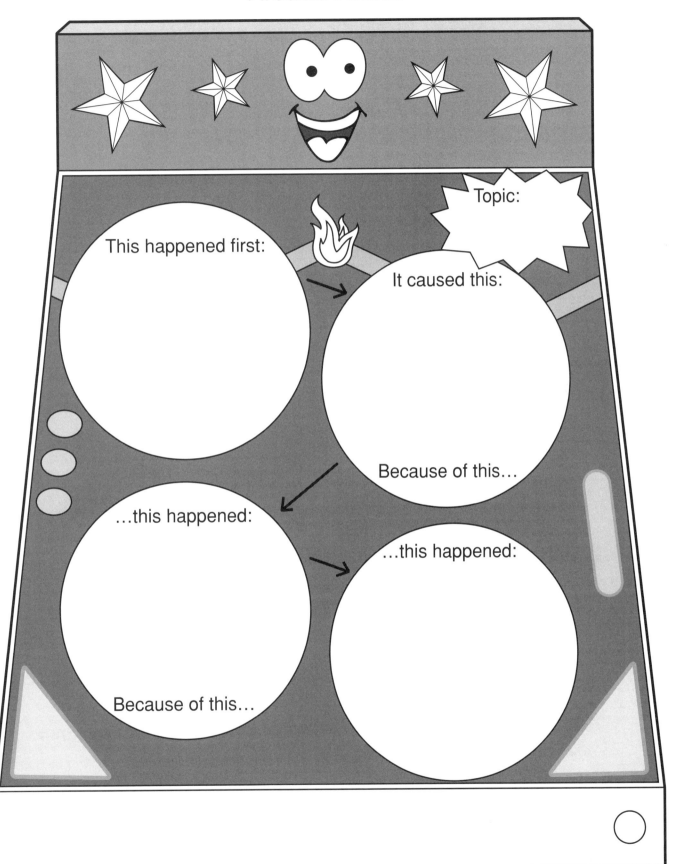

Topic:

This happened first:

It caused this:

Because of this…

…this happened:

Because of this…

…this happened:

Flying Free

Venn diagram

Directions for completing page 71:

Label each blank with an item to compare. Then record the similarities between the two items in the inner section and the differences in each outer section.

Building Skills:

Writing: After completing the graphic organizer, have each student use the information to write a **comparison paragraph**.

Reading: Have small groups of students use the organizer to **compare two different versions of the same fairy tale.**

Math: Create a transparency of the organizer and use it to **compare solid figures.**

Flying Free

item _____

item _____

Different

Alike

Different

Big Top Fun

T chart

Directions for completing page 73:

Write the topic and related items on the lines provided. Then compare the two items in each column.

Building Skills

Reading: Have students use the organizer to compare the **strengths and weaknesses of a character.**

Reading: Use the organizer to create a class list of **facts and opinions** about a story or chapter book being read in class.

Social Studies: Have students use the organizer to compare the **pros and cons** of something happening in their school or community.

Name _____

Big Top Fun

topic

related item

related item

Compare and Contrast **73**

Capture the Castle

H Chart

Directions for completing page 75:
   Write the topic and two ideas to be compared in the spaces provided. On the castle, write how the two ideas are similar and different.

Building Skills

Reading: Have each student use the organizer to **compare and contrast two characters** from similar stories.

Science: Have small groups of students use the organizer to **compare how variations in an experiment** affect the outcome.

Social Studies: Use the organizer to discuss the similarities and differences between two **historical figures.**

Capture the Castle

Topic:

Idea:

Idea:

Both:

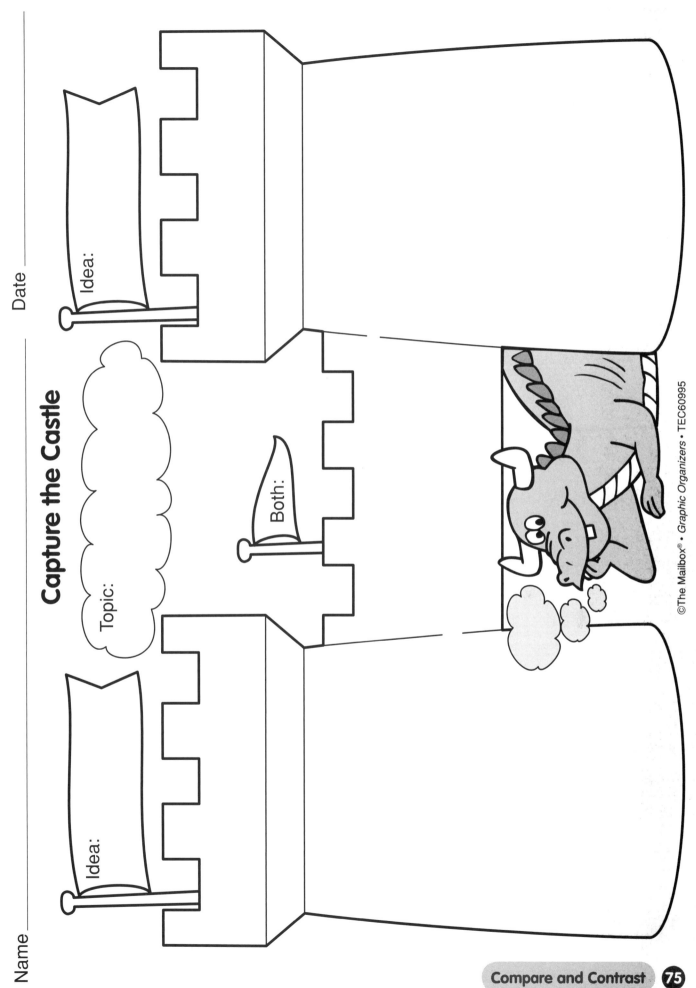

What a Catch!

Compare-and-contrast map

Directions for completing page 77:

1. Write the topic on the bat.
2. On each hat, write the name of each person or item being compared.
3. In each ball and mitt, write information comparing and contrasting the two items or people.

Building Skills

Reading: Have each student use the organizer to **compare and contrast the plots** in two different stories.

Reading: Use the organizer to **compare and contrast two characters** in a book or story.

Social Studies: Display a transparency of the organizer. Use the organizer to help students **compare their community or town** to a larger (or smaller) community or town.

Name_____ Date _____

What a Catch!

Topic: _____

item/person   item/person

⟷

⟷

⟷

Piecing It Together

Comparison grid

Directions for completing page 79:

Write the two titles being compared in the spaces provided. Then compare the setting, characters, and main problem of the two reading selections.

Building Skills

Reading: Have each student use the organizer to **compare two stories** by the same author.

Writing: Use the organizer to help students **plan a twist to a familiar fairy tale or folktale.** Have each student write the name of the familiar tale in the first title box. Have him write the title of the twisted tale in the second title box. Next, have the student complete the remaining sections to plan out the differences for the new version. Once the organizer is complete, have the student use the information to write his twisted tale.

Social Studies: Have small groups of students use the organizer to **compare two informational articles** or current events newspaper articles.

Name _____

Piecing It Together

| Title 1 | Title 2 | Similarities | Differences |

Setting:

Characters:

Problem:

©The Mailbox® • Graphic Organizers • TEC60995

Colorful and Fluttery

Word, definition, and picture chart

Directions for completing page 81:

1. Write the word on the butterfly's body.
2. Write a definition of the word.
3. Draw a picture that goes with the word.
4. Write on the flower petals other words that the word reminds you of.

Building Skills

Writing: Have students practice their **challenging spelling words** by completing a different organizer about each one.

Reading: Have students use several copies of the organizer to make a **dictionary of multiple-meaning words.**

Social Studies: Introduce new **social studies vocabulary** words by having groups of students complete an organizer about each one.

Name _____ Date _____

Colorful and Fluttery

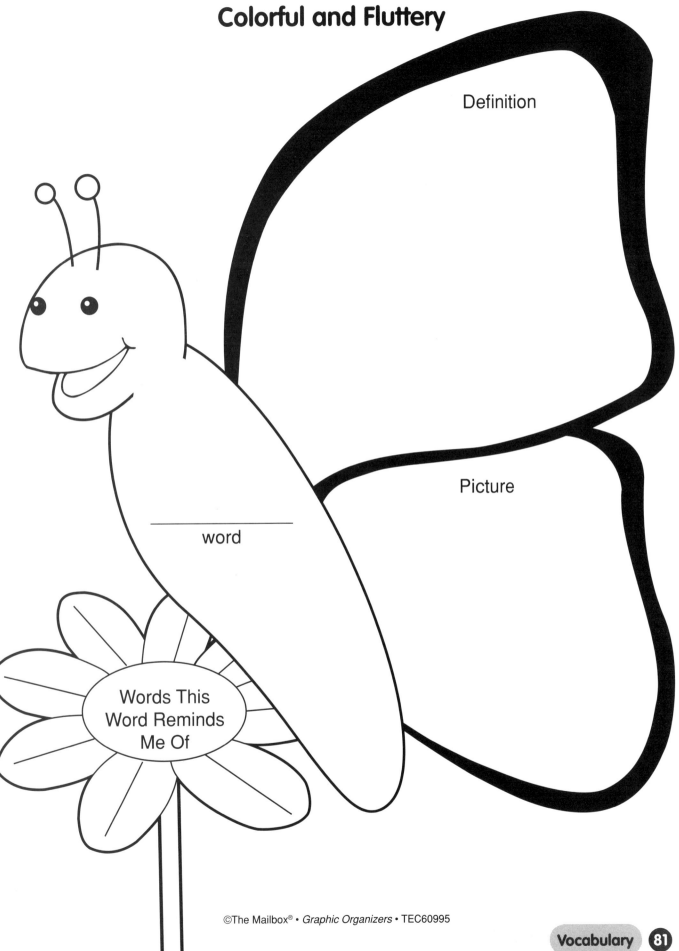

Definition

Picture

word

Words This Word Reminds Me Of

Out of This World!

Word web

Directions for completing page 83:

1. Write the word.
2. Write your own definition of the word.
3. Write the dictionary's definition of the word.
4. Complete the sentence by describing something the word reminds you of.
5. Draw a picture that goes with the word and its meaning.

Building Skills

Math: Have students staple several copies of the organizer together to make a *glossary of math terms.*

Science: Have students use copies of the organizer to learn new *science vocabulary* when beginning a new unit.

Social Studies: Direct students to use the organizer to *make and adjust predictions* about vocabulary when beginning a new unit.

Name

Date

Out of This World!

word

I think the word means this:

The dictionary says the word means this:

Here's a picture of the word:

The word reminds me of

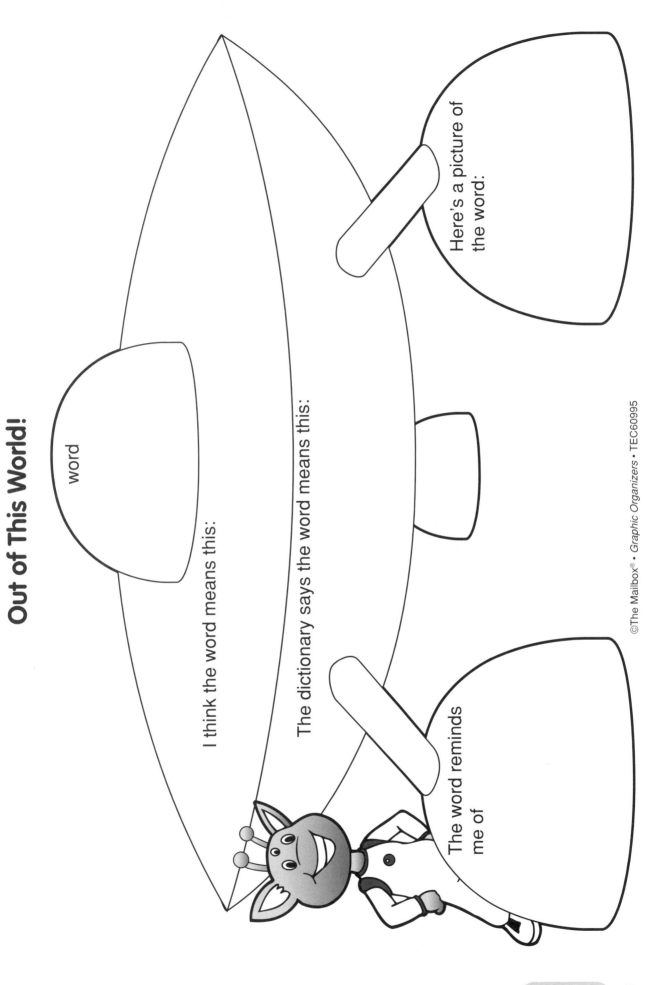

A Hive Full of Clues

Context clue chart

Directions for completing page 85:
1. Write the unfamiliar word.
2. Write the page number where the word is found.
3. Write clues that may help you understand the meaning of the word.
4. Write a definition for the word in your own words. If there are not enough clues to help you define the word, write the dictionary's definition of it.

Building Skills

Reading: Have students use the organizer to determine the meanings of unfamiliar words when reading a *poetry selection.*

Reading: Have students use multiple copies of the organizer to make a *chapter book glossary.* Display the glossary and chapter book together in the class library.

Social Studies: Have students use the organizer to determine the meanings of *social studies vocabulary* when beginning a new unit.

Name _____

Date _____

A Hive Full of Clues

word _____

Page:

Context Clue:

Context Clue:

Definition:

word _____

Page:

Context Clue:

Context Clue:

Definition:

©The Mailbox® • *Graphic Organizers* • TEC60995

Vocabulary 85

It's in the Bank!

Spelling practice chart

Directions for completing page 87:

1. Write a spelling word on each piggy bank.
2. Check the spelling of each word. Fix any mistakes. Color the "Check" coin.
3. Study the spelling of each word. Color the "Study" coin.
4. Cover the spelling word on the bank while you write it on the dollar box.
5. Check what you have written. Fix any mistakes. Color the "Final Check" coin.

Building Skills

Writing: Have students use the organizer to practice *"challenge" words* they'd like to save for later writing activities.

Reading: Have students use the organizer to study words from a single *word family, root word, or phonemic structure.*

Science: Have students use the organizer to study *key vocabulary words* during a science unit.

Name _____

It's in the Bank!

Study   Check   word   Final Check   word

Study   Check   word   Final Check   word

Study   Check   word   Final Check   word

Study   Check   word   Final Check   word

Study   Check   word   Final Check   word

Study   Check   word   Final Check   word

Roping in Words!

Spelling chart

Directions for completing page 89:

1. As your teacher reads each spelling word aloud, write it in the first column.

2. Later, check each spelling word by looking it up in the dictionary. Fix any mistakes. Put an X in the "Check" box as you check each word.

3. Study the word by writing it three times, spelling it in your mind three times, or spelling it out loud three times. Put an X in the "Study" box after you study each word.

4. Fold the paper back along the "Study" line. Have a parent or friend call out each spelling word. Rewrite each spelling word in the second "Word" column.

5. Unfold the paper and check your work. Put an X in the "Check" box as you check each word.

Building Skills

Spelling: Have students use the organizer as a **pretest and posttest** for spelling words.

Writing: Have each student use several copies of the organizer to make a **personal dictionary.**

Social Studies: Have students use the organizer to learn **vocabulary words** for a new social studies unit.

Roping In Words!

Word	Check	Study	Word	Check	Study

Cool Treats

Directions for completing page 91:
Write a question about the topic in the top ice pop. After reading or research, write the answer to each question in the bottom ice pop.

Building Skills

Reading: To *set a purpose for reading,* have a student program each top ice pop with a specific question about the next chapter in the book he's reading. Then have him read to find and record the answer to each question.

Science: Assign each student a topic related to the current science unit. Have each student use the organizer to *write four questions about her assigned topic.* Then have her research each question, collecting data to help her write an answer for the question.

Social Studies: Program a copy of the organizer with *four questions about a current events issue* in your community or state. Give one copy of the programmed organizer to each student. Then have the student interview an adult and ask him each question on the organizer, recording the adult's response. Have students share and compare their findings.

Name _____

Cool Treats

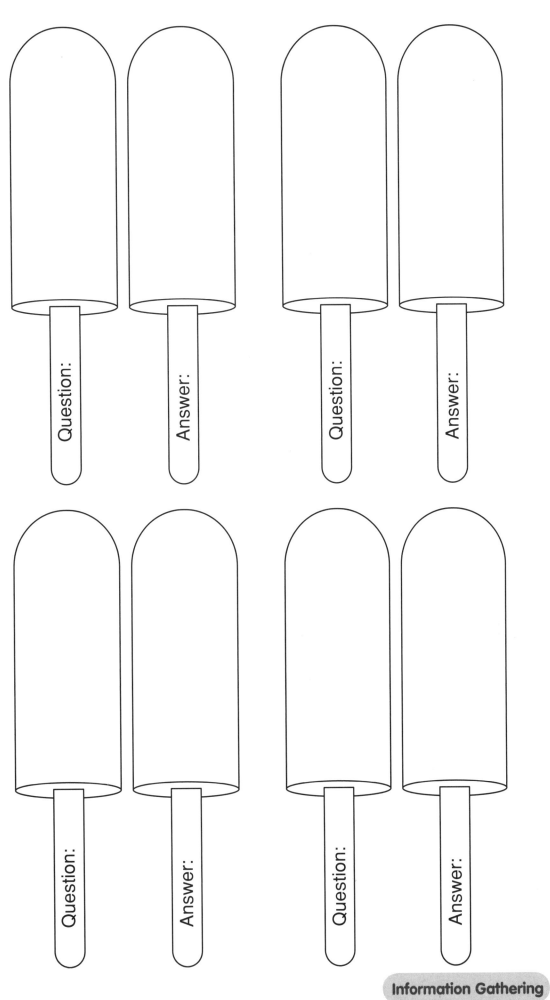

Question:

Answer:

Question:

Answer:

Question:

Answer:

Question:

Answer:

©The Mailbox® • *Graphic Organizers* • TEC60995

Spouting Off!

SQ3R chart

Directions for completing page 93:

1. Survey: Scan the reading selection, paying attention to text features such as pictures, headings, and captions. In the space provided, write down important titles and subtitles you find.
2. Question: In the space provided, write questions you have about the text.
3. Read: Read the text. Answer each question in the space provided.
4. Recite: In the space provided, write a few key words, phrases, or facts that will help you retell what you have read.
5. Review: Write a summary of your findings.

Building Skills

Reading: Assign each pair of students a different picture book to read. Have each pair use the organizer before, during, and after reading to **build comprehension skills.**

Science or Social Studies: Have students use the organizer before, during, and after reading an informational text to help them better **understand key concepts.**

Name _____ Date _____

Spouting Off!

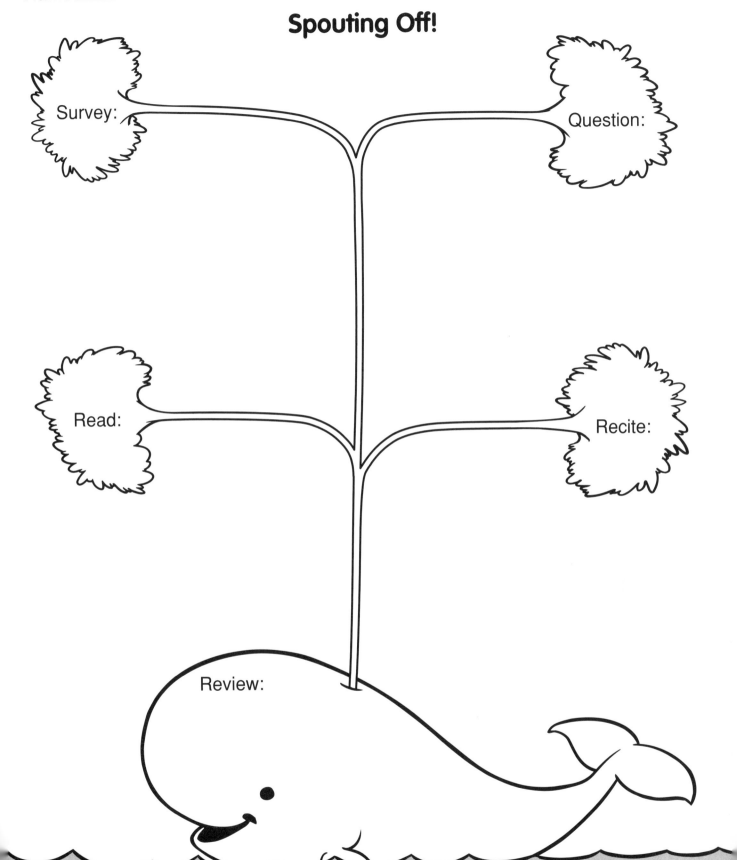

Survey:

Question:

Read:

Recite:

Review:

On the Sidewalk

Five senses chart

Directions for completing page 95:
    List four items or places to be explored. Write about how each one looks, smells, feels, tastes, and sounds.

Building Skills

Writing: Have students use the organizer to **add details** to their **descriptive writing.**

Reading: Use the organizer to help students **make notes** about what a character experiences in a picture book or chapter book.

Science: Have students use the organizer during specific units of study or during **experiments related to the five senses.**

Name

Date

On the Sidewalk

Item/Place	Looks	Smells	Feels	Tastes	Sounds

©The Mailbox® • *Graphic Organizers* • TEC60995

Hop on Over!

Information web

Directions for completing page 97:

1. Write the main topic or title on the frog's lily pad.
2. Write related ideas or subtopics on each blank of the other lily pads.
3. Underneath each idea, record key facts, words, or phrases about the idea or subtopic.

Building Skills

Writing: Use the organizer to help students **create topic headings** before they begin to write a book report.

Science: Have students use the organizer to help **collect their thoughts and data** for a science report.

Social Studies: After reading a social studies selection, have students use the organizer to **identify the subtopics** related to the topic of study.

Hop on Over!

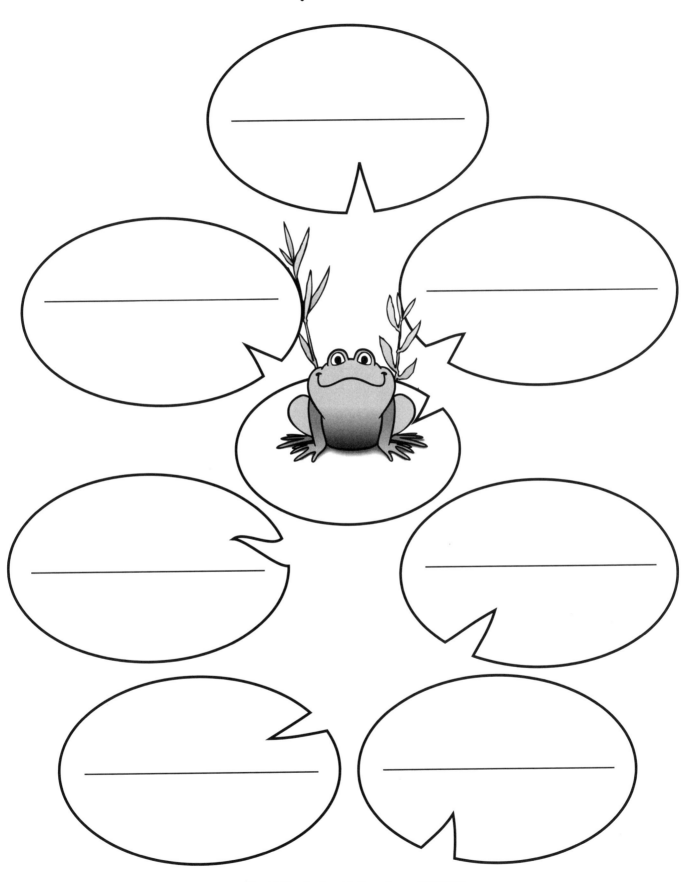

Light Up My Life

Personal history timeline

Directions for completing page 99:

1. Write the person's name at the bottom of the lantern.
2. Write their birthdate at the top of the lantern.
3. Choose seven life events to feature on the lantern. Write the date of each event on the line provided.
4. Write a brief description about each event in the space provided.

Building Skills

Social Studies: Have students use the organizer to *summarize* the highlights of their lives from birth to the present.

Social Studies: Direct each student to interview a staff member, such as the secretary, cafeteria manager, or custodian. Then have her use the organizer to *create a timeline* of the staff member's life.

Social Studies: Have each student interview a family member. Then have him use the organizer to *highlight the key events* in the relative's life.

Light Up My Life

Birthdate: _____

Date: _____

Date: _____

Date: _____

Date: _____

Date: _____

Date: _____

Date: _____

Life of

Badge of Honor

Coat of arms

Directions for completing page 101:

1. Draw an illustration of the featured person in the center box and write his or her name on the blank.
2. Think of four topics to share information about this person. Write each topic in a separate numbered box.
3. Write or illustrate information about each topic in the space provided.

Building Skills

Reading: Use the organizer to have each student *create a character coat of arms.* Have her select a character from a book she is reading. Then have her use the organizer to share information about the character's family, personality, likes and dislikes, etc.

Social Studies: Have each student use the organizer to *create a personal family coat of arms.*

Social Studies: Use the organizer at the beginning of the year as an icebreaker to *help students get to know each other* better. Pair students. Direct the students in each pair to interview one another. Then have each student use the organizer to create a coat of arms about her partner.

Name _____ Date _____

Badge of Honor

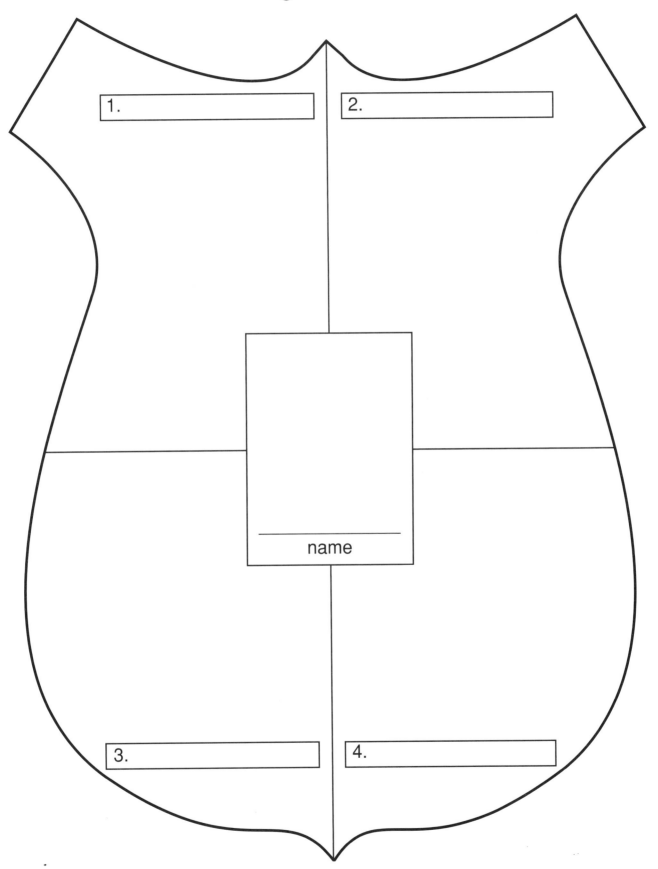

1.

2.

name

3.

4.

Let's Talk About Me!

Personal attribute web

Directions for completing page 103:

1. Write your name on the sign that says, "Featured Speaker."
2. Imagine that you are giving a speech about yourself as you complete the sentence on each speech bubble.
3. Draw features on the speaker so that it resembles you.

Building Skills

Reading: Use the organizer to **explore a character** in a chapter book.

Social Studies: Have students use the organizer to **explore a historical character.**

Social Studies: Direct students to use the organizer to **introduce themselves to their classmates.**

Name _____ Date _____

Let's Talk About Me!

I was born…

In my family…

One of my favorite…

I feel worried when…

My next goal is…

I am very good at…

People don't know this about me…

One day I'll be remembered for…

Featured
Speaker:

_____

_____

Milk and Cookies

Decision-making chart

Directions for completing page 105:

State the problem on the first glass of milk. Then use each additional glass of milk to record important information needed to solve the problem.

Building Skills

Reading: Have each student use the organizer to *predict how a character might solve a problem* faced in a story.

Math: Use a transparency of the organizer to help the class reach a *reasonable solution to a word problem.*

Social Studies: Have small groups of students use the organizer to *plan a solution* to a school or community issue.

Milk and Cookies

The Problem

Important Information

My Thinking

What I Need to Know

What I Found Out

My Decision

Howdy, Partner!

Problem-solving grid

Directions for completing page 107:

1. Write the main problem.
2. Write two possible solutions.
3. Write the pros and cons of each solution listed.
4. Write your solution to the problem.

Building Skills

Reading: Have small groups of students use the organizer to *analyze* how a character solved a problem in a story and to *compare* how they would have solved the problem.

Science: Direct a student to use the organizer to help him determine which of two experiments would be best for a *science fair project*.

Social Studies: Have each student use the organizer to decide how to *respond to a bully*.

Name _____

Date _____

Howdy, Partner!

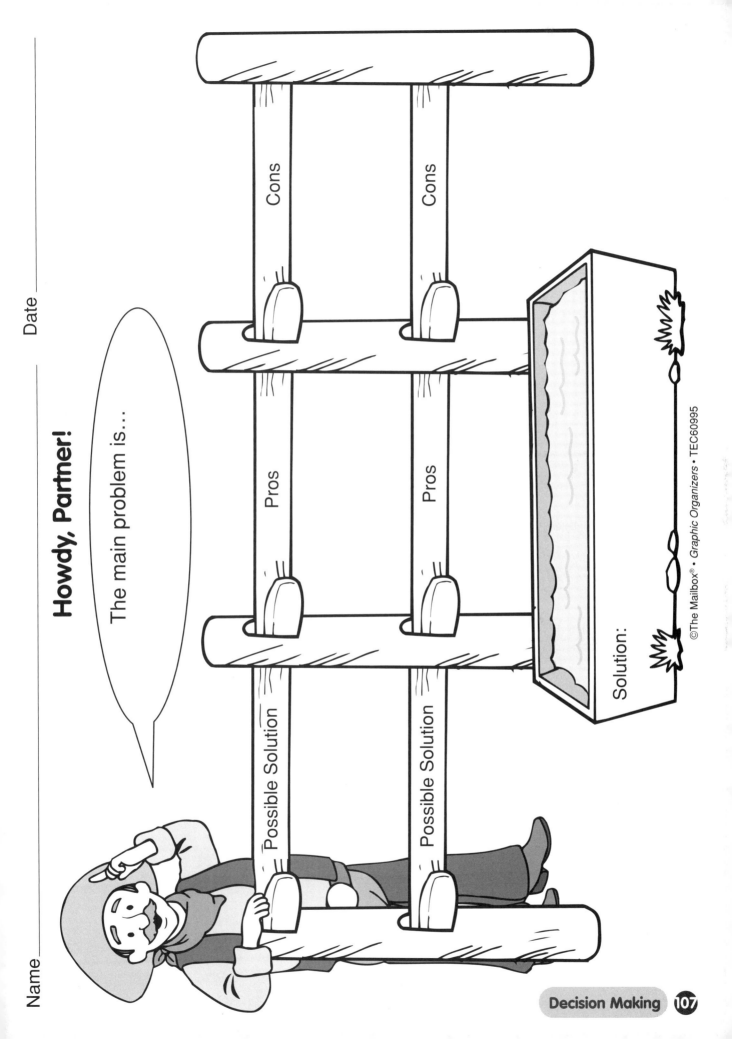

The main problem is...

Cons

Cons

Pros

Pros

Possible Solution

Possible Solution

Solution:

©The Mailbox® • *Graphic Organizers* • TEC60995

Going for the Goal

Goal-planning chart

Directions for completing page 109:
   Write the goal in the center of the ball. Next, write the steps or tasks needed to accomplish this goal in the remaining sections of the ball.

Building Skills

School: Have students use the organizer to plan how to achieve a **school-related goal,** such as improving their grades, doing better in a particular subject area, mastering their multiplication facts, or reading more books than they did the previous year.

Personal: Have students use the organizer to plan how to achieve a **personal goal,** such as earning money for something they want to buy, becoming more physically fit, or keeping their rooms clean.

Name_____ Date _____

Going for the Goal

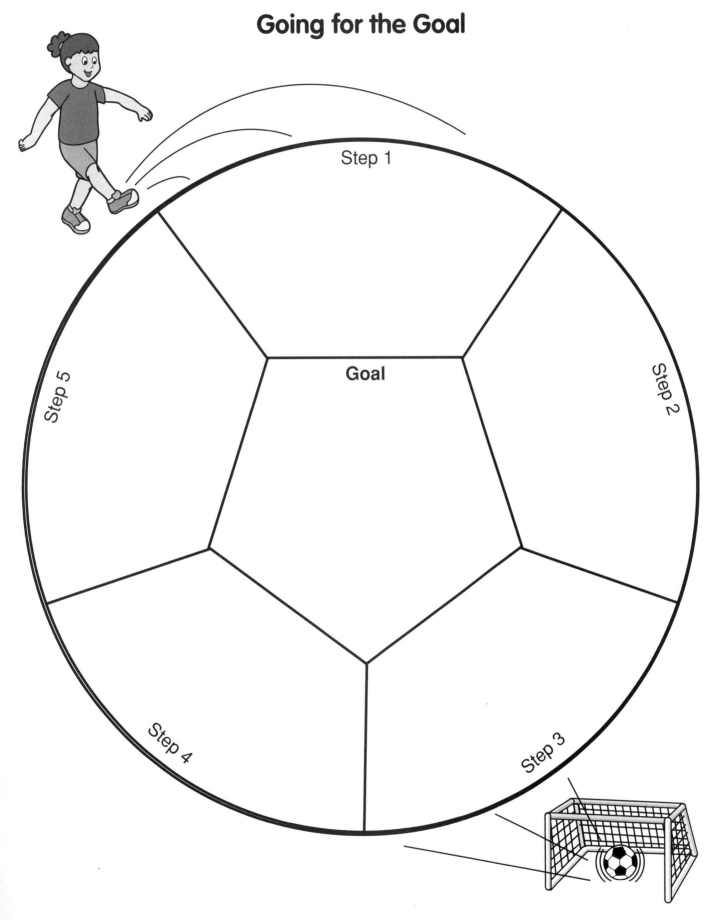

Step 1

Step 2

Step 3

Step 4

Step 5

Goal

Building a Project

Project-planning chart

Directions for completing page 111:

1. Write the problem or question that is the topic of the project.
2. Brainstorm project ideas.
3. Choose a project and write it in the project box.
4. List the resources you will need.
5. Describe the experiment or project.
6. List the materials you will need.
7. On the gate, create a timeline for the project.

Building Skills

Reading: Show students how to use the organizer to **plan a project for a chapter book** or picture book.

Science: Have students use the organizer to plan a **science fair project.**

Social Studies: Have students use the organizer to **plan a project** about a person or an event from history.

For a handy homework log, see page 112!

Name _____

Date _____

Building a Project

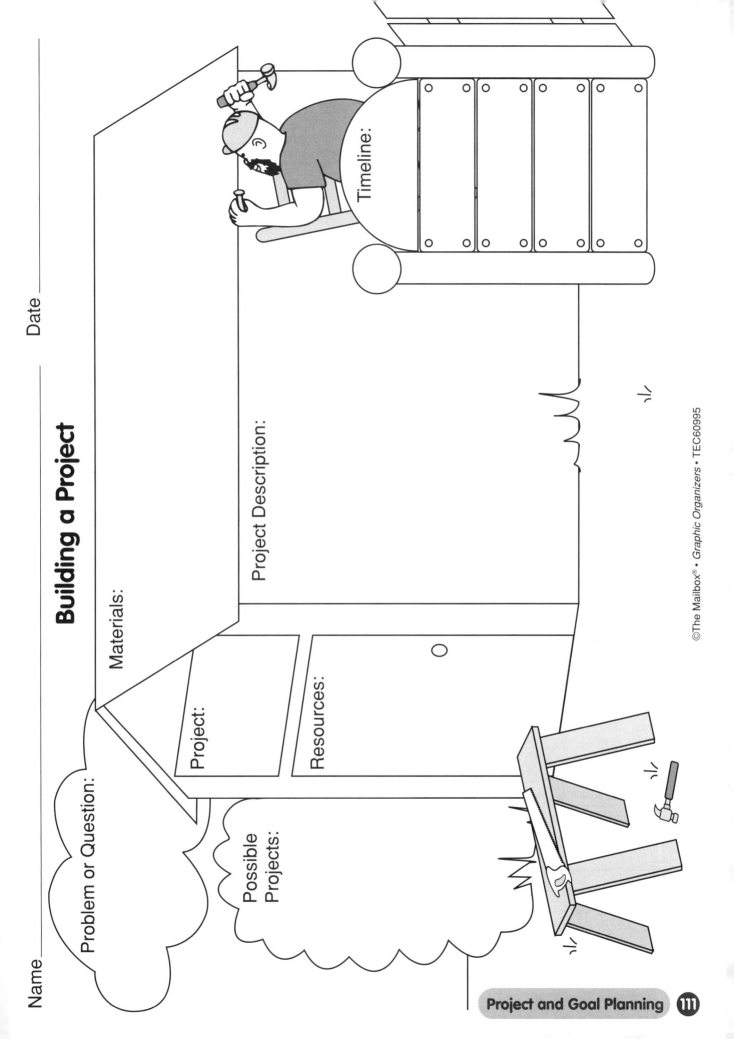

Problem or Question:

Materials:

Project:

Project Description:

Resources:

Possible Projects:

Timeline:

_____'s

Homework Log

Monday		_____ date
Tuesday		_____ date
Wednesday		_____ date
Thursday		_____ date
Friday		_____ date

Things to Bring to School:

Other Reminders:

©The Mailbox® • *Graphic Organizers* • TEC60995

112 **Project and Goal Planning**